ONE MILLION MONARCHS

By Dawn Leon

Illustrated by Taera Harman

Lilly George Publishing

For my husband, Brent
Thank you for all of your support in making this time-consuming book.
I love you.

For Eli, Chloe, Erin, and Caleb
May all of you spread your wings and soar through this adventure we call life.
I love you.

- Dawn Leon

For John David and Miriam Thomson
Thank you for your brilliant minds, selfless hearts, and constant inspiration.

- Taera Harman

For our mother, Shirley
Thank you for bringing us the butterflies. We love you.

For our Uncle Butch
Fly high...

One million monarchs roost in trees,
waiting for warmth to set them free.

They flutter and soar to journey forth,
with the magical force that pulls them north.
They soon need fuel and begin to slow,
to rest their wings in the fields below.

Where are the flowers when they land?
Gone from chemicals made by man.
Hungry for nectar and find nothing but lawn,
too tired to fly,
some monarchs are gone.

One thousand monarchs try to set forth,
with the magical force that pulls them north.
They land to rest on weary legs,
to take a drink and lay their eggs.

Where is milkweed for eggs to hatch?
We don't like weeds so we mow the patch.
Too weak to open their wings and soar,
some monarchs land and are no more.

One hundred monarchs journey forth,
with the magical force that pulls them north.

The fields are full of corn and beans,
flowers and milkweed cannot be seen.
Some cannot fly another day,
the monarchs land and forever stay.

One little monarch in my tree.
She is all alone then she meets...

ME!

I give her milkweed, I give her a flower.
She lays her eggs and gains her power.

I watch her babies grow to be
beautiful monarchs
to find YOUR tree!

You can help a monarch in need.
In your yard drop a milkweed seed!

If you give them your love and a garden to tend we'll have **one million monarchs** once again!

Dawn Leon is a labor and delivery RN in Davenport, Iowa. She also raises monarch butterflies and gives lectures on how all of us can do our part to protect this beautiful pollinator.

Dawn is married to husband, Brent, and has four children.

Besides being a nurse and a Mommy, Dawn enjoys singing, reading, writing, and gardening.

"There are two things I never get tired of seeing: the birth of a new human being, and the birth of a new butterfly."
– Dawn Leon

Please visit thecaterpillarchronicles.com for more information o raising monarch butterflies.

Taera Harman is an artist / illustrator. She Graduated from the Minneapolis College of Art and Design with a Bachelor of Fine Arts degree. Her artwork has been displayed in Starbucks, US Bank, and numerous galleries in her area.

Taera teaches art classes at the University of Iowa Belin-Blank Center, and has designed art summers for the Montessori Children's Garden.

Taera is a world traveler and enjoys nature photography.

Please visit her Facebook page:
Artwork by Taera Harman

Made in the USA
Coppell, TX
02 September 2021